Opal Whiteley's Beginning

Sunrise of a Child Naturalist

&

Hoops & Hoopla

Diary of Hardwood Hell

ALSO BY DAVID H. ROSEN

Opal Whiteley's Beginning

Sunrise of a Child Naturalist

&

Hoops & Hoopla

Diary of Hardwood Hell

by DAVID H. ROSEN

RESOURCE *Publications* • Eugene, Oregon

OPAL WHITELEY'S BEGINNING
Sunrise of a Child Naturalist

&

HOOPS & HOOPLA
Diary of Hardwood Hell

Resource Publications
An Imprint of Wipf and Stock Publishers
199 W. 8th Ave., Suite 3
Eugene, OR 97401

www.wipfandstock.com

PAPERBACK ISBN: 978-1-5326-6085-6

Manufactured in the U.S.A.   09/17/18

Contents

"Be tough in the way a blade of grass is: rooted, willing to lean, and at peace with what is around it."

—NATALIE GOLDBERG

Opal Whiteley's Beginning

Sunrise of a Child Naturalist

Prelude

Earth, ourselves,
breathe and awaken,
leaves are stirring,
all things moving,
new day coming,
life renewing.

Pawnee Prayer

THIS PAWNEE PRAYER REMINDS one of Opal Whiteley. She was a naturalist and child memoirist. *The Story of Opal: The Journal of an Understanding Heart,* published serially in *The Atlantic Monthly,* was a bestseller a century ago. Before her popular book was published, Opal had been a student at the University of Oregon in 1916. In all accounts of her, she was short in stature, dark with long braided hair, and appeared to be of Native American descent.

Opal Whiteley
University of Oregon archives

Opal Irene Whiteley was born on December 11, 1897 in Colton, Washington. In her memoir, Opal maintained that she was an orphan. Her parents, Ed and Lizzie, claimed that this was not true. The following is a work of historical fiction that imagines Opal's origins.

OPAL WAS CONCEIVED ON a clear, early Autumn day in a mossy lea near a forest. Her father, Ed, was a lumberjack. On one of his excursions into the nearby hills east of the Snake River, Ed was surveying trees to cut for a new cabin. He was tall, strong, and fair-skinned. Deep in the woods, he sat down to have his lunch, which his wife Lizzie had made. It consisted of homemade bread, two apples, and a bit of cheese. Ed and Lizzie had decided to settle in Colton where the fertile hills meet the prairie north of the Snake River. Ed had learned to be in the wild as a young boy and his father had taught him to hunt with a bow and arrow.

Ed found a huge tree to cut down for lumber. After sawing for hours, he was exhausted, so he lay down. To his surprise, he had slept for several hours.

When he stirred and got up, he could see through the trees a woman who was taking a bath in a nearby creek-fed pool. He was very quiet because he didn't want to disturb her. She had tied her Appaloosa horse to a tree. He wondered whether she was a member of the Palus people, part of the Sahaptin tribe. He noticed her long, black braids and her beautiful dark, smooth skin.

Suddenly, a few leaves cracked beneath his feet, and the woman turned and looked right at him. He gazed at her big, brown eyes. Fortunately, he had learned a few words in the Nez Perce language and said, "Hello."

Afraid and embarrassed, she sank below the water. He awkwardly said, "Sorry to bother you."

She was shocked, but spoke in broken English, "Who are you?"

Assuming she couldn't understand rapid English, Ed spoke slowly: "My name is Ed. I live with my wife Lizzie on the prairie near Colton. I came here to find a tree so we can build a bigger cabin for our planned family."

The woman responded, "I am Pula."

Ed then said, "I'll go back and have my lunch so you can have some privacy."

He returned to the mossy area where he left his uneaten lunch. He sat down with his back to Pula and started eating. 'She is such a beautiful young maiden,' he thought. Images of Pula streamed through Ed's mind. After finishing his meal, he drank water from a stream below. He turned and saw that Pula had gotten dressed. He went over again to say that he was sorry for disturbing her. Then he offered her one of his apples. Pula accepted it and thanked him.

"Would you care to eat your apple with me," he asked.

"That would be fine," she responded.

They sat down and each took a bite of their apples.

"This is delicious," Pula said.

"Yes," Ed agreed, "we grow them ourselves."

Ed asked if Pula was married, like him.

"No," Pula said, "I'm the Chief's daughter, and he will pick a husband for me."

Ed responded, "I've met your father before. In fact, I may have even seen you in the background. My father was trading horses with him for some cattle."

Pula said, "Yes, I remember this."

"Have you ever met my wife, Lizzie? You may have seen her in the general store."

"I don't think so," Pula said.

Then Ed shared something private. He asked whether Pula could keep a secret.

She said, "Yes."

Ed stated, "It's sad to say this, but Lizzie is unable to conceive a child. We've been trying unsuccessfully for five years."

Ed's eyes were wet with tears. Pula saw that he was a sensitive man. Then she did something impulsive. She took her finger and wiped the tears from Ed's eyes. Ed was taken aback, but he could not help seeing Pula's soul in her beautiful eyes. She was so close that he embraced her. Then they rolled over on the moss and kissed passionately. They started taking their clothes off and one thing led to another.

After heated love-making, they discussed what had happened. Both were embarrassed, but they felt an intense fondness for one another.

"We shouldn't have let this happen," Pula said. "What do I tell my father?"

"What do you mean," Ed responded, "you don't need to tell him anything."

Ed insisted, "Please don't tell him, he'd kill me."

Pula said, "My father cares about people, and he would never harm you."

"But wouldn't he be upset?"

"Yes, he would be."

Ed said, "We're in the soup together, and we're just going to have to deal with it."

Pula asked, "What do you mean?"

Ed responded, "Let's just see what happens. Shall we meet again here?"

Pula nodded.

After a month went by, Pula and Ed met again.

Ed offered her another apple.

"How are you," he asked.

"Fine," she said, "You were right, Ed, my father doesn't know."

They agreed to meet a third time in a couple of weeks.

When Pula arrived, Ed noticed that she was worried.

"What's wrong," he asked.

She said "I'm pregnant."

Ed saw that Pula's eyes were wet with tears.

He embraced and comforted her.

Ed consoled Pula, "It's okay, we will figure this out together."

"What about Lizzie?"

Ed responded, "I'll talk with her about what happened."

"Wouldn't it bother her?"

Ed said, "Yes, but I hope she'll forgive me."

Pula realized that she too would have to confront the truth.

After a hug, they parted.

When Pula saw her father, she tearfully said, "I have something difficult to tell you."

"What is it?"

"I'm going to have a baby."

"Who is the father," the chief asked.

"He is a white man. His name is Ed and I think you know his father."

The chief said, "This is terrible news. I already have a husband for you. You've disgraced yourself, me, your mother, and our people."

He was furious. "How dare you!"

Pula, with her head down, whispered, "I have a plan. The man and his wife are unable to have a baby. I will give this child to them."

With tears running down his face, the chief tenderly said, "I love you. But, you must keep out of sight. I'll arrange a hut for you stay in. Our people can never know about this. It must remain a secret."

Later Pula relayed her plan to Ed.

Distressed, but relieved, Ed agreed with her idea.

That evening he sat down with Lizzie.

Hesitantly, he said, "I have something to tell you. You remember when I was going up to the hills to get wood for our new cabin? Well, I met the chief's daughter there. I feel horrible. This should have never happened. I've spoken with our pastor about it, and he said I needed to tell you and ask for forgiveness."

Lizzie demanded, "What happened?"

Ed choked, "I was unfaithful with her. A baby will be born. However, she has agreed to give the baby to us."

Lizzie began to cry. "I cannot love a child that's not my own."

Ed argued, "But isn't this a gift from God?"

Lizzie remained silent.

Six months passed.

Pula gave birth to a beautiful baby girl. She was tiny and dark-skinned.

The baby remained nameless until Pula took her to Ed.

Sadly, she said, "I can't keep this baby and remain in my tribe. Now, you and Lizzie have a daughter."

Ed responded reluctantly, "I will take our daughter, but I want you to help me name her. She is lovely, just like you. I can see the resemblance."

"Thank you, Ed. That's very kind. What shall we name her?"

Ed noticed a small opal pendant around Pula's neck. "Because she is precious, let's call her Opal."

"Opal is a beautiful name. This necklace was given to me by my father's mother."

Pula handed the baby over to Ed.

He began to cry as he took Opal.

"Lizzie wanted to name her Irene, but that can be her middle name."

He and Pula embraced and held Opal together.

"I know this is a most difficult time. You are an angel for giving us this gift."

Pula remained silent while tears streamed down her cheeks.
Ed and Pula went their separate ways.

While riding away on her horse, Pula was enchanted by thoughts of her future husband and home.

Hoops & Hoopla

Diary of Hardwood Hell

Prelude

THIS IS A TRUE story about my experience as the center on the 1962-63 Shimer College basketball team that set a national record of 37 straight losses.

OUT OF HIGH SCHOOL, I was accepted to the University of Southern California. When I went there, I was overwhelmed by its size and living conditions. The dorms were huge and impersonal. I decided to explore the fraternities as they were smaller and supposedly better. However, when I went to the first frat rush party, I was aghast. The amount of alcohol and drunkenness shocked me. I was also shown exam files and told that if I came to their frat house, I'd get an A average. They asked what my major would be and I said "pre-med." They guaranteed that I'd get into medical school. I felt sick to my stomach.

All this caused me to leave as soon as possible and to seek the total opposite in higher education. After just two weeks, I dropped out of USC and went to Shimer College in Mount Carroll, Illinois, which was known to have a true educational environment. Most of the faculty were from the University of Chicago. Going to Shimer College had its high-points and low-points. It was a Great Books school. Going from

20,000 students to 300 was refreshing. I found what I was looking for.

An added benefit resulted when I tried out for the basketball team. The coach, "Shep," was an alcoholic. There were twelve spots on the team and twelve people tried out. I remember our first meeting with Shep in the locker room. Coach said, "There are two strict training rules that you must adhere to." Having been a high school basketball player, I knew this was coming. Shep quickly got our attention. He held up one finger and said, "There will be no smoking in the opposing team's locker room." Then, he held up two fingers and said, "Number two: there will be no drinking in the opposing team's locker room." Shep then took out a silver flask from his sport coat and took a sip.

A wealthy donor had given the school a nice bus and uniforms for the basketball team in exchange for accommodating his mentally challenged son to attend the college indefinitely.

Our schedule was demanding. In the 1962–63 season, we played such schools as Clinton College, George Washington College, University of Illinois at Chicago, and Eureka College, where President Reagan went. I'll never forget on our trips to these schools, Shep had a prior arrangement with the bus driver to pull into a tavern outside of the town. When we entered the bar, Shep would say, "Set 'em up for my boys. Just one drink. No hard liquor, just a beer. It will help them relax and get ready for the big game."

One time in a blizzard, Curt (one of three people who had played high school basketball) fell into a snow drift and passed out. Shep slapped him to wake up. Then he told our trainer, "Get the ammonia salt and oxygen to get Curt back in shape for the game." It worked! Curt and the other guard, Rick, were ready to play ball.

In one of our practice sessions, Rick asked Shep about his playbook. Shep said, "Well, I don't have one." Curt and I both responded, "Shep, you need to have at least one play." Then, he invented one on the spot. "I got it! It's called 'Rosie.' Curt, either you pass to Rick or Rick passes to you, and the one that doesn't pass goes and screens David's man. Then the one who has the ball passes it to David and he shoots." I said, "Shep, my name is Rosen, don't you think they would catch on?" Shep said, "I doubt it."

I remember vividly jumping center with a 6'8 African American from the University of Illinois at Chicago and touching his armpit. At just over 6 feet, I was the tallest player on our team.

One of our players was not even 5 feet tall. His uniform was so big that it would drag on the floor when we warmed up. Shep wanted everyone to play and despite his issues, he was very kind. He even put Eric, someone who had never played basketball, into games. Eric was repeatedly called out by refs for double-dribbling. Another player, approaching Shep's age, had a big stomach and would quickly accumulate more fouls than points.

At half time during one of our games, we were only a few points behind. Shep entered the locker room with his exhausted team and said: "I'm not even gonna smoke or drink because we could actually win this one." We were surprised to hear such an enthusiastic remark. We were laboring for breath and knew it was impossible. Soon Shep would know what we knew, as the opposing team ended up quadrupling our score. Nevertheless, our solo cheerleader, a girlfriend of one of the players, waved her pom pom and cheered me on as I scored 23 points. On the way back, we never argued with Shep's desire to have a drink. Some of us even had a second and third.

When we played against Eureka College, it was like a television show. They had a band, cheerleaders, and fans watching the game. All we had was one struggling cheerleader and good uniforms. I recall the half time with Shep being agitated and smoking excessively. He kept saying, "I know you can play better than this." I thought to myself, 'Shep, how would you know? You're in your ninth year of a PhD program in physical education.'

You can see why we lost 37 straight games, which became a national record. It was held for almost 50 years until Towson College broke it with 41 losses. When we set the record, the basketball team hoisted Shep on our shoulders and carried him through the dining hall while the students and faculty cheered.

It was crystal clear that Shimer was not known for its athletics. It was a scholastic institution. While I was a student there, Aldous Huxley came to give a lecture. He met with students and faculty at the President's house. Huxley was an erudite and brilliant man. After meeting him, I decided to read *The Doors of Perception* and *Brave New World*.

I'll never forget Huxley talking about Greece, its history, and its mythology. At that moment, I decided to visit that country. I acted on this desire and left Shimer College after one year. I had applied to The Experiment in International Living and was accepted to live with a family in Greece.

Leaving Shimer ended my illustrious career as an inter-collegiate basketball player. At the end of our notorious season, the following picture of Shep was in *The Chicago Tribune*. The last I heard, Shep had moved to Alaska to teach at a junior college, and yes, coach basketball.

Coach Shep
Chicago Tribune

www.ingramcontent.com/pod-product-compliance
Lightning Source LLC
Chambersburg PA
CBHW051051030426
42339CB00006B/302